HAPPY TO BE ME !
A SONG ABOUT FRIENDSHIP

By VITA JIMÉNEZ

Illustrations by JANET CHEESEMAN

Music by ERIK KOSKINEN

CANTATA
LEARNING

WWW.CANTATALEARNING.COM

CANTATA
LEARNING

Published by Cantata Learning
1710 Roe Crest Drive
North Mankato, MN 56003
www.cantatalearning.com

A note to educators and librarians from the publisher: Cantata Learning has provided the following data to assist in book processing and suggested use of Cantata Learning product.

Publisher's Cataloging-in-Publication Data
Prepared by Librarian Consultant: Ann-Marie Begnaud
Library of Congress Control Number: 2016938057
    Happy to Be Me! : A Song about Friendship
    Series: Me, My Friends, My Community
    By Vita Jiménez
    Illustrations by Janet Cheeseman
    Music by Erik Koskinen
    Summary: Positive, upbeat lyrics and colorful illustrations teach children to celebrate their differences while accepting others.
    ISBN: 978-1-63290-777-6 (library binding/CD)
Suggested Dewey and Subject Headings:
    Dewey: E 155.2
    LCSH Subject Headings: Individual differences – Juvenile literature. | Friendship – Juvenile literature. | Individual differences – Songs and music – Texts. | Friendship – Songs and music – Texts. | Individual differences – Juvenile sound recordings. | Friendship – Juvenile sound recordings.
    Sears Subject Headings: Individuality. | Friendship. | School songbooks. | Children's songs. | Popular music.
    BISAC Subject Headings: JUVENILE NONFICTION / People & Places / General. | JUVENILE NONFICTION / Music / Songbooks. | JUVENILE NONFICTION / Social Topics / Friendship.

Book design and art direction: Tim Palin Creative
Editorial direction: Flat Sole Studio
Music direction: Elizabeth Draper
Music written and produced by Erik Koskinen and recorded at Real Phonic Studios

Printed in the United States of America in North Mankato, Minnesota.
072017   0367CGF17

ACCESS THE MUSIC!

SCAN CODE WITH MOBILE APP

CANTATALEARNING.COM

TIPS TO SUPPORT LITERACY AT HOME

WHY READING AND SINGING WITH YOUR CHILD IS SO IMPORTANT

Daily reading with your child leads to increased academic achievement. Music and songs, specifically rhyming songs, are a fun and easy way to build early literacy and language development. Music skills correlate significantly with both phonological awareness and reading development. Singing helps build vocabulary and speech development. And reading and appreciating music together is a wonderful way to strengthen your relationship.

READ AND SING EVERY DAY!

TIPS FOR USING CANTATA LEARNING BOOKS AND SONGS DURING YOUR DAILY STORY TIME

1. As you sing and read, point out the different words on the page that rhyme. Suggest other words that rhyme.

2. Memorize simple rhymes such as Itsy Bitsy Spider and sing them together. This encourages comprehension skills and early literacy skills.

3. Use the questions in the back of each book to guide your singing and storytelling.

4. Read the included sheet music with your child while you listen to the song. How do the music notes correlate to the words of the song?

5. Sing along on the go and at home. Access music by scanning the QR code on each Cantata book. You can also stream or download the music for free to your computer, smartphone, or mobile device.

Devoting time to daily reading shows that you are available for your child. Together, you are building language, literacy, and listening skills.

Have fun reading and singing!

Bullies sometimes **tease** the people who don't look the same as they do. This kind of teasing is mean and **hurtful**. If you are being teased, tell the bully to stop. Tell that person the world would be **boring** if we all looked the same!

Now turn the page and sing about how you are happy to be you!

4

My ears, your ears,
different but the same.

My ears, your ears,
don't call my ears a name.

6

My ears are very special.
My ears **belong** to me.

My ears are very special.
I'm happy to be me.

My nose, your nose,
different but the same.

My nose, your nose,
don't call my nose a name.

My nose is very special.
My nose belongs to me.

My nose is very special.
I'm happy to be me.

9

My teeth, your teeth,
different but the same.

My teeth, your teeth,
don't call my teeth a name.

My teeth are very special.
My teeth belong to me.

My teeth are very special.
I'm happy to be me.

My feet, your feet,
different but the same.

My feet, your feet,
don't call my feet a name.

My feet are very special.
My feet belong to me.

My feet are very special.
I'm happy to be me.

13

My body, your body,
different but the same.

My body, your body,
don't call my body a name.

My body is very special.
My body belongs to me.

My body is very special.
I'm happy to be me.

My skin, your skin,
different but the same.

My skin, your skin,
don't call my skin a name.

16

My skin is very special.
My skin belongs to me.

My skin is very special.
I'm happy to be me.

My hair, your hair,
different but the same.

My hair, your hair,
don't call my hair a name.

18

My hair is very special.
My hair belongs to me.

My hair is very special.
I'm happy to be me.

I'm very special.
I'm happy to be me.

I'm very special.
I'm happy to be me.

I'm very special.
I'm happy to be me.

I'm very special.
I'm happy to be me.

21

SONG LYRICS
Happy to Be Me!

My ears, your ears,
different but the same.
My ears, your ears,
don't call my ears a name.

My ears are very special.
My ears belong to me.
My ears are very special.
I'm happy to be me.

My nose, your nose,
different but the same.
My nose, your nose,
don't call my nose a name.

My nose is very special.
My nose belongs to me.
My nose is very special.
I'm happy to be me.

My teeth, your teeth,
different but the same.
My teeth, your teeth,
don't call my teeth a name.

My teeth are very special.
My teeth belong to me.
My teeth are very special.
I'm happy to be me.

My feet, your feet,
different but the same.
My feet, your feet,
don't call my feet a name.

My feet are very special.
My feet belong to me.
My feet are very special.
I'm happy to be me.

My body, your body,
different but the same.
My body, your body,
don't call my body a name.

My body is very special.
My body belongs to me.
My body is very special.
I'm happy to be me.

My skin, your skin,
different but the same.
My skin, your skin,
don't call my skin a name.

My skin is very special.
My skin belongs to me.
My skin is very special.
I'm happy to be me.

My hair, your hair,
different but the same.
My hair, your hair,
don't call my hair a name.

My hair is very special.
My hair belongs to me.
My hair is very special.
I'm happy to be me.

I'm very special.
I'm happy to be me.
I'm very special.
I'm happy to be me.

I'm very special.
I'm happy to be me.
I'm very special.
I'm happy to be me.

Happy to Be Me!

Indie Pop
Erik Koskinen

1. My ears, your ears, dif-ferent but the same. My ears, your ears, don't call my ears a name.

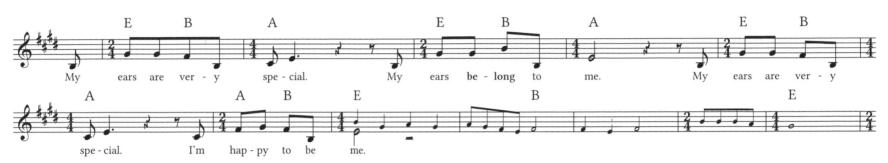

My ears are ver-y spe-cial. My ears be-long to me. My ears are ver-y

spe-cial. I'm hap-py to be me.

Verse 2
My nose, your nose, different but the same.
My nose, your nose, don't call my nose a name.

My nose is very special. My nose belongs to me.
My nose is very special. I'm happy to be me.

Verse 3
My teeth, your teeth, different but the same.
My teeth, your teeth, don't call my teeth a name.

My teeth are very special. My teeth belong to me.
My teeth are very special. I'm happy to be me.

Verse 4
My feet, your feet, different but the same.
My feet, your feet, don't call my feet a name.

My feet are very special. My feet belong to me.
My feet are very special. I'm happy to be me.

Verse 5
My body, your body, different but the same.
My body, your body, don't call my body a name.

My body is very special. My body belongs to me.
My body is very special. I'm happy to be me.

Verse 6
My skin, your skin, different but the same.
My skin, your skin, don't call my skin a name.

My skin is very special. My skin belongs to me.
My skin is very special. I'm happy to be me.

Verse 7
My hair, your hair, different but the same.
My hair, your hair, don't call my hair a name.

My hair is very special. My hair belongs to me.
My hair is very special. I'm happy to be me.

I'm ver-y spe-cial. I'm hap-py to be me. I'm ver-y spe-cial. I'm hap-py to be me.

me.

GLOSSARY

belong—something that is yours

boring—not interesting or fun

hurtful—upsetting to someone

tease—to make fun of someone

GUIDED READING ACTIVITIES

1. Imagine that everyone else looked just like you. How would that make you feel? What problems would that cause?

2. Sit down with one of your friends. List the ways you look the same. Then write down how you look different. Why is it good that we all look different?

3. Draw a picture of yourself. You can use a mirror to see what you look like while you are drawing.

TO LEARN MORE

Dewdney, Anna. *Llama, Llama and the Bully Goat.* New York: Viking, 2013.

Doering, Amanda. *Insults Aren't Funny: What to Do about Verbal Bullying.* North Mankato, MN: Capstone, 2016.

Higgins, Melissa. *Teasing Isn't Funny: Emotional Bullying.* North Mankato, MN: Capstone, 2016.

Higgins, Melissa. *We All Look Different.* North Mankato, MN: Capstone, 2012.